How To Plan A Pinterest-Worthy Party WITHOUT DYING
(or losing your chill)

AMY LAURENS

OTHER WORKS
Find other works by the author at
http://www.amylaurens.com/books/

How To Plan A Pinterest-Worthy Party WITHOUT DYING (or losing your chill)

AMY LAURENS

Inkprint PRESS
www.inkprintpress.com

Copyright © 2018 Amy Laurens

All rights reserved. No part of this book may be reproduced in any form or by any electronic or mechanical means, including information storage and retrieval systems, without permission in writing from the publisher, except by a reviewer, who may quote brief passages in a review.

YOU HAVE THE LIMITED RIGHT TO PRINT THE WORKSHEETS INCLUDED IN THIS BOOK FOR YOUR OWN USE. YOU MAY NOT SELL THEM OR GIVE THEM AWAY WITHOUT THE EXPLICIT WRITTEN PERMISSION OF THE AUTHOR.

Cover design © Amy Laurens.
Interior photographs © Amy Laurens.

Thanks, Mum.

INTRODUCTION

It can feel like there's a lot of pressure sometimes to host 'perfect' events, what with the advent of Pinterest and Instagram and the like. My family is Big on Events, and we can Pinterest party like it's... uh, 2018.

I've been involved in plenty of events-coordination that took weeks and even months of planning, and my sisters, mother and I have collaborative Pinterest boards spawning out our ears.

But let's face it: My life is packed. I don't have TIME to hold Pinterest events. And honestly? I tried one for my birthday a while ago when I turned 30 and... eh.

I mean, don't get me wrong, it was amazing. It's just that the sheer amount of work co-ordinating on the day meant I was pretty stuffed by the time the party actually *started*.

Also, many of the "events" I'm doing these days are for kids, and you know what? A three-year-old doesn't care if you spent six hours on their party or one or twelve.

They just love that it's a party.

But! It is entirely possible to get a party worthy of Pinterest and Instagram WITHOUT dying, losing your chill, and making you want to stab your eyeballs out by the time the party arrives. All it takes is a little bit of planning…

PART ONE: THE PREP

Honestly, 90% of success in anything is the preparation you put in. The secret to hosting a Pinterest-worthy party isn't really in what you do on the day; it's in what you plan beforehand.

But party planning is really, really easy to lose hours of your time in. You dive into Pinterest, and before you know it half the day is gone. That's not an efficient way of planning a party, and it's not a recipe for keeping your chill when you have a zillion other competing demands on your time.

So let's spend some time laying the groundwork: before you even get to planning the specifics, there's some important preparation to do.

STEP 1: FOCUS

The first really important step is to figure out which bit of partying you actually enjoy. My middle sister loves decorating. My mum loves cooking.

Me? I love the cake. (Okay shush those of you who read my blog, I can hear your shock and surprise from here :P) So for me, that's my deal-breaker: everything else I can hack, but the cake needs to be top-notch.

Figure out that one thing that is make-or-break for you as far as an awesome, wow-factor party is concerned.

It is having the entire room full of themed decorations?

It is an incredible, awe-inspiring cake?

It is having every item of food totally in theme?

Or is it something else entirely?

STEP 2: IDEA KERNEL

Okay, now that you know what's important to you focus-wise, it's time to brainstorm ideas.

Chances are you or the person you're planning for has this bit covered for you: my son requested a Toy Story party for his birthday in 2017.

(Incidentally, "Toy Story" is too big a kernel for a keeping-yourself-alive party, so we narrowed it down further: Buzz was his favourite character, so we'd be having a Buzz focus.)

In 2018, it was pirates, with a clear focus on 'treasure island' rather than skull-and-cross-bones (which helpfully let me weed out a LOT of ideas that were cool, but just didn't fit).

Figuring 2017 was the last year I'd really get to steer the party-theme ship for the baby, I decided to do narwhals, because NARWHALS, Y'ALL.

However, when we discovered that she was totally obsessed with cows about two months out, I flipped and we went with cows instead.

(Still hoping to convince her to do narwhals at some point...)

It's important that you hone in on that one specific thing is that you're interested in, because it helps when it's time to...

STEP 3: BRAINSTORM

While you can totally do this months ahead (and I do because I like to get things sorted during school holidays so term time is less frenetic), you do run the risk of having to flip if the person's interest changes (especially with kids).

Of course, you can always say, "Tough luck!" Your call.

What you DON'T want to be doing, though, is planning the night before. Har. But with that said, if you use this system you could easily pull off a low-stress, Pinterest-worthy party with only a week's planning, if you can either do everything yourself or have people you can outsource to.

It took me maybe an hour to totally plan the pirate treasure party, and if I'd been so inclined, I could have done all the prep in the week before, even around work (though it would have meant a week of nothing but work + party prep).

So what exactly do you plan? EVERYTHING, but usually in a specific order.

First of all, hold onto your idea kernel. It's going to be your guiding light when you come across ideas that are shiny but ultimately distracting.

Secondly, brainstorm. I do this on Pinterest because it's a great way to generate a lot of ideas *fast*, and you don't have to do the thinking because you can pretty much be guaranteed that someone out there has already done it for you.

Alternatively, you could do image searches on Google; you'll still get some good results, it's just more of a pain to try to save them and they might not be as strictly relevant.

So what am I searching for? Anything around my idea kernel. For the Toy Story party I searched 'Toy Story cakes', 'Buzz Lightyear cakes', 'Toy Story party', 'Toy Story food', etc.

Often on Pinterest you can luck out and find that someone's helpfully put together some composite images that show the food, the decorations, and the cake all in one; these can be a great place to look for ideas, especially for food.

For the baby's party, you can see some of the key ideas reproduced below. Bearing in mind that the first pins are at the bottom, you can see the gradual drift in ideas: my idea kernel was narwhals with mermaids in a teal-and-purple colour scheme, so down the bottom of the board are a lot of mermaidy pins with purple and teal colour-schemes.

However, as I went along you'll see that the pins drift towards silver + blue + Arctic. I had this thought that since it was a winter party and narwhals are Arctic I could incorporate that...

But because I had my idea kernel, I realised I was drifting away from what I really wanted, and knew it was time to stop brainstorming.

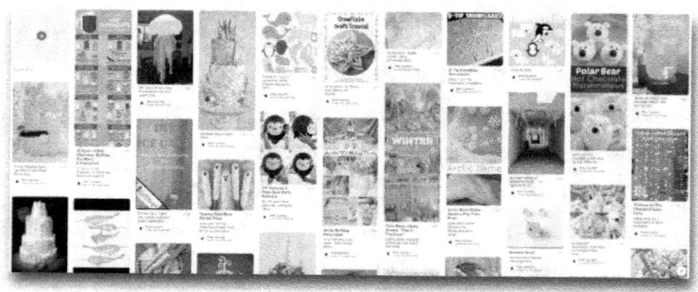

When I was re-brainstorming for the cow party, I knew I'd be looking at a lot of farm party things—but because I knew I wanted to focus specifically on *cows*, I could avoid getting distracted by all the cute general-farm-themed stuff out there, and it literally took 15 minutes to put together a pretty huge board. Same with the pirate treasure party.

(see:

www.pinterest.com/inkylaurens/cow-party
www.pinterest.com/inkylaurens/pirate-party).

You know it's time to stop brainstorming either when you find yourself repeating a lot of ideas, or when you start to drift away from your kernel. You can get a perfectly decent brain-storm done in 10-15 minutes.

PART TWO: THE PLANNING

Now we finally get to the actual planning ☺ But this time, we're not in danger of it eating years of your life, because we've laid our ground-work: we know what our specific idea kernel is, we've done a brainstorm. We have both the possible and the container in which to fit the plausible. So let's get planning!

STEP 4: DECORATION

Having done your initial brainstorm, you'll have come across some things that you're definitely keen on implementing—food ideas, decorations, maybe activities too. Hold onto all this; we'll go through it one thing at a time.

First: decorations. Because I am prone to falling in love with far too many ideas, and the whole point of this process is to keep things fast and contained, I like to do a quick table sketch, because it immediately shows me that I'm trying to pack too much in—it won't all fit on the table!! :D (And yes, make sure to allow plenty of room for food!)

You can see my decoration sketch for the narwhal party below, and also my sketch for the cow party. The annotations on the narwhal party sketch are colour suggestions for the jellyfish, while the annotations in the cow party, starting from top left and moving anticlockwise, are:

- fabric ties in pink, green and cowprint
- dessert
- white cloth
- cow garland
- soup
- basket of bread
- use white vase

- farm animal cookies (circles)
- pop on mini haystack?

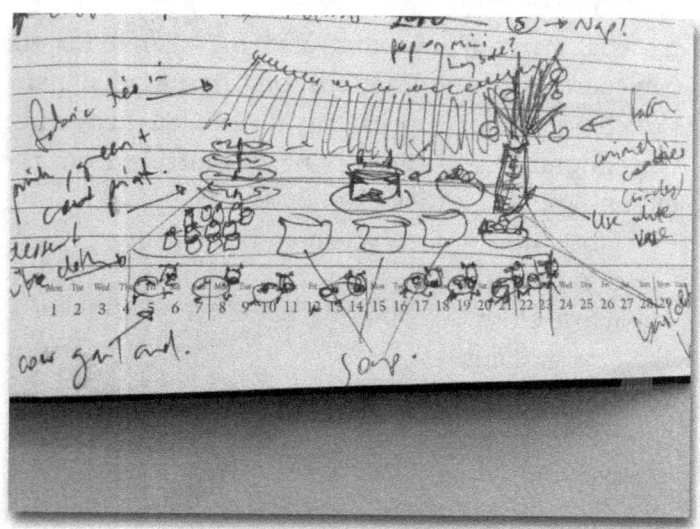

I didn't do one for the Toy Story party because it was down at the local park—the only decorations I had were labels for the food/ drinks. I also have one for the pirate treasure party, but I ended up raiding my sister's props cupboard and found a whole bunch of things, so a lot of things changed from that initial plan (though the layout stayed basically the same).

Now, unless decorations are your FOCUS item (and honestly, even if they are), this is where things can spiral out of control and stress you out. The internet has SO many great ideas that look AMAZING—but let's be honest: most of them look amazing because the person either paid a fortune for them, or spent years of their life on them.

Having planned seven kids' parties of my own now and been involved in a host of others, my rule of thumb is that magic number is THREE, as in you only really need THREE key decorations to bring things together.

And while if decorations are your focus item, you might want to decorate the whole room, for the rest of us, honestly? Just decorate the table. Make one corner of the room special, and you can pretty much ignore the rest, or just fill it with balloons and/or streamers in your theme colours.

(Or, another handy idea for warm-weather parties, we set up a gazebo tent in the backyard—encourages food to be consumed outside, so less mess to worry about, and provides a contained area for decorations: the gazebo gets decorated and I'll maybe stick something on the front door, and *that's it*. Contained = keeping you alive.)

From my sketches, you can see my three key items:
- a backdrop on the wall behind the table,
- a decorative item on the table to give height and drama, and then
- small decorations across the front of the table.

Narwhal party: "snowflakes" as the back-drop, silver branches with sea stars on the right back of the table for height/drama/wow factor, and a couple of jellyfish across the front.

Cow party: tied-fabric-strip garland across the back as the backdrop, naked branches for height/drama, and a cow garland across the front of the table.

I made the cow garland the other night and it took a grand total of 30 mins while I was watching TV, and even then only because the cutting out was fiddly (I could have chosen an easier shape).

Pro tips here: see how the image I chose has a nice, thick, black border around it?

That's wriggle room for cutting so you don't have to be so careful about cutting *exactly right*.

Further pro tips? If you look closely at some of the cows, you'll see how neatly I did NOT cut them out, but literally no one is going to notice this except you, because they'll be focused on the food on the table. On the flip side, a lot more people will notice if you lose your chill ;) :) :D

Treasure party: originally I was going with bubbles for the backdrop with the intent of reusing them for the future narwhal party (yes, I am campaigning hard :D); after raiding my sister's props cupboard, this was changed to an actual printed-scene backdrop, and some paper circle-fan things in different blues (so bubble-*ish*).

The height was going to be provided by a tree of stacked pineapples in the centre of the fruit salad, but my sister had blow-up palm trees that served the same function for zero cost, and while I was going to make portholes to string across the front of the tables, the fabric maps my sister had worked just as well for zero effort. Yay survival and not losing our chill, right? :)

And yes, this concept works for adult parties too. I didn't really think about it consciously when I decorated for my sister's baby shower, but the same principles were there:
- Backdrop: tree branches and a literal 'backdrop' of vines and fairy lights on the table;
- Height: branches, the cake elevated on top of the fish tank (!), chopping boards on inverted bowls etc, and bunches of flowers to give varied height across the tables;

- <u>Front element</u>: further vines, branches and fairy lights across the front of the table on the floor.

Exactly the same principles, and yet it made the entire room feel utterly magical.

STEP 5: MENU

Before you plan the menu, figure out:
1) how many people you're feeding,
2) how much time you have to cook, and
3) how many people you have to help you cook.

The Toy Story party had a more extensive menu because my amazing mum volunteered (okay I begged and pleaded just a little) to make like 20 pizzas for it.

The baby's parties, in both 2017 and 2016? Soup. Soup and bread, because I am cooking and it's mid-winter and even these 'family-only' parties are about 25 people and soup is QUICK and EASY, and easy to scale up.

Even the pizza for the Toy Story party was comparatively easy, because Mum could make them way ahead and freeze them. You do NOT want to be stuck doing major food prep on the day of the party, trust me on that one. That is almost a guaranteed way to lose your chill and end up dead.

(Which nearly happened at the Toy Story party, because I failed to connect the dots when it came to having to heat the pizzas in the (small!) oven at home, and then transport them a block down to the park...)

So I tend to opt for one main savoury dish that is quick, easy, can be prepped ahead and is easy to scale up—pizza, soup, etc.

Figure you need one main dish like your pizza or soup, and maybe 2-3 accompaniments (though I'll be honest, all I accompany soup with is a variety of breads—I do use 2-3 varieties still though, so similar concept?).

The same for dessert: if you're serving cake, PLEASE serve it as your key dessert, because otherwise you WILL be left with acres and acres of cake that will see you through to the next family birthday! :D So, like savouries, figure cake + 2-3 accompaniments.

Which brings you to the only other food-related decision you have to make: to theme or not to theme! Because we're all about maintaining our chill here, do what works for you.

BUT, because we're only decorating the table, and because why let something do one job when it could do two, I do tend to theme at least some of my food, because then it counts as extra decorations ;) But you totally don't have to, and you don't have to theme all of it (see: soup, and also: chill).

For the Toy Story party (which, note, I have four accompaniments for each course because I had help with cooking!):

Main savoury: pizza, which becomes Pizza Planet pizza of course.

Accompaniments: "Camouflage salad" (just green-leaf salad with a variety of leaf colours, referring to the army men in the movie), "Slinky Dog pasta" (pasta salad with spiral pasta), "Sheriff badges" (cheesy puff pastry stars—referring to Woody), and "Mr Pricklepants pull-apart garlic bread" (get a loaf of bread, cut it into inch squares but not through the base, douse it in garlic butter, wrap in foil and bake).

Main dessert: Buzz Lightyear-inspired rocket cake in banana (birthday boy's choice)

Accompaniments: "Cowgirl trail mix" (with lots of lollies and chocolate, of course, referring to Jessie), "Hamm's Portraits" (pig-face-shaped meringues), "Green Aliens" (cups of green jelly with three meringue eyeballs on top for the Pizza Planet aliens), and "Potato-head Cupcakes" (DIY cupcake decoration—triple bonus: food, decoration AND an activity for the kids!).

Drinks: sweet herbal tea (TEA-rex), water (rocket fuel) and banana milkshake (moo juice).

For each of these I just had a little banner on a toothpick with a picture of the character and the name of the food, and voila! That was the decorations for the entire party.

For the narwhal party I wasn't going to theme at all, because I was literally going to do just soup and cake (I did this in 2016 for her first birthday), but now it's a cow party I am actually going to do a couple of themed desserts.

The main dessert is cake, obviously, but I did circular chocolate brownies for 'cow pats' (totally gross but Mr 5 LOVED it); and planned to do round sugar cookies with animal faces (the most time-consuming thing, but the plan was to organise my time so that the only things I was doing in the two days up to the party would be these cookies and the cake).*

* Turns out piping faces with royal icing is a lot harder than it looks, so I downscaled: I made cowprint sugar cookies: round cookies covered with plain white royal icing and then with brown patches piped on with dark chocolate. I also ditched hanging them from the branches and just piled them in a glass dish!

For the pirate treasure party I kept things really simple, a) because of how much leftover food there was at the last summer kids' party,* and b) because I was actually working through this process this time (from the worksheets! They do actually work!) which made it easier to keep it contained.

* Spoiler: there was still a LOT of food left over. Like, 8 or 10 pizzas. I wish I was kidding.

Main savoury: treasure map pizzas (took about 2-3 hours with two of us the night before, but we also had literally twice as many pizzas as required, and it was FUN making them. Big deal: if it's not fun, don't spend so much time on it!)

Accompaniments: Crab croissants (which ended up just being croissants because I ran out of care-factor), seaweed dip with octopus, vegetable tree with crudités, and chips.

Main dessert: CAKE. Of course.

Accompaniments: fruit salad, sugar cookies (shaped as starfish and sand dollars*), and pirate gold (various gold-wrapped or yellow-coloured chocolates and lollies).

Drinks: iced water, tropical juice, and blue Gatorade mixed with lemonade as 'sea water'.

* Another hot tip: DELEGATE, and get over it if it doesn't look perfect. I got husband + a friend of his who was staying just before the party to supervise the kids making the sugar cookies (I'd made the dough two days earlier). They LOVED cutting out the cookies and making them (the kids that is, HA), and were SUPER proud on the day that they had contributed ☺

STEP 6: CAKE

No secrets: this is my favourite part :D But even if it isn't yours, don't stress! It doesn't really take that much planning at all.

First questions first: How many serves will you need, what flavour/s do you want, and what design will you use? This is where your brainstorming can prove handy—you might already have some cake ideas in mind, but if not, you have a tightly-defined idea and you've already thought of your decorations, so you can quickly come up with something that fits in.

Consider: What is the absolute narrow focus of your party? Would that be a good idea for a cake?

For example, I ended up with a cow cake, a rocket ship, and a treasure chest, all direct reflections of the very core of the party's theme.

Alternatively, you could think about what aspects of the focus your other decorations/food already have covered; is there another aspect you haven't conveyed yet that could work as the cake?

Planning sketches…

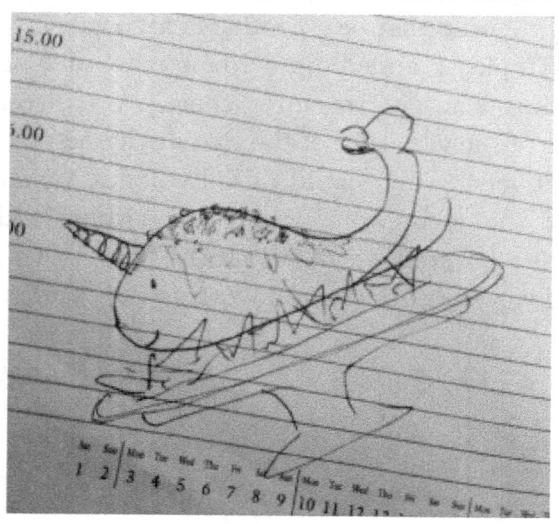

The next thing to consider is who will be making the cake, and what your budget is. If you're getting someone else to bake it, make sure to book as far ahead as you can so they can plan.

If you're making the cake, these are the steps you'll need to take:

1) Figure out the specifics of your design and flavours, including which recipes you'll be using and how much you need to make.

Don't forget to take into account how much time you have: for the treasure chest cake, I originally planned to go all-out and do a woodgrain, hand-painted fondant cake. Then I realised that I was holding this party the weekend after school started back, meaning I'd have not a lot of time OR energy that week... and it was for a six-year-old.

So instead, I went with the plain chocolate buttercream version in the picture at the end of this section—and the birthday boy was extremely happy, and I was happy with it too, AND I didn't die trying to get everything done :)

(Start to finish I think decorating the cake only took me about an hour!)

2) Make a shopping list, not only of ingredients (for cake, icing, and possibly filling), but also of all the decorative items you want to include.

For the treasure chest cake, I wanted a 'six' topper, which I ordered for about $12 from Etsy. Planning the cake and making the list early ensured I had enough time to order this before the party.

3) Diarise! Plan when you're going to shop (and always allow enough time to go BACK to the shop closer to the party in case you forget something—this is something I have to specifically plan, as there are only two or three specialty cake stores in town, and some of them have very limited opening hours, and all of them have different ranges of stock). Then diarise when you're going to bake: unless it's a light and fluffy cake, you can often make it up to a month beforehand and freeze it!

I usually bake the cake the weekend before I need it, freeze it for a few nights, and pull it out with two nights to go. (This works well for me as I'm often baking mud cakes, and they freeze like a dream; I once had a family member freeze one of my filled mud cakes for six months, and when it was defrosted it still tasted fresh!)

Finally, diarise when you're going to decorate the cake. Since we usually do Sunday parties in our household, I tend to reserve Saturday late afternoon/evening for cake decorating.

Most designs will hold up just fine overnight in the fridge, and fondant designs (which <u>must</u> be stored *out* of the fridge so the fondant doesn't sweat) can easily sit for a couple of days or more.

Below are the cakes I've done for the last four parties (no, that's not the narwhal up first, that's an angler fish, which was the baby's first birthday cake because Reasons). You'll note they all have one thing in common: a slightly haphazard decorating style while allowed me to really easily cover any 'mistakes'.

STEP 7: INVITATIONS

At this point, you've already had to think a couple of times about how many people you're inviting, so now's the time to crystallise that. Make your guest list, remember that the point here is *keeping your chill and not dying*. Don't go overboard on the guests unless there is literally no other way around it!

Unless invitations happen to be your focus area, there's really no point spending money on them these days. Consider digital invites: you can get great access to free or nearly-free invitations through websites like PaperlessPost (which will also track RSVPs for you—this is the site I use), and you can also make them yourself for free on websites like Canva.

If you're making them yourself, you could always browse somewhere like PaperlessPost first for ideas. When you're done, simply download your image, and email it out to everyone. (Or, if you really want to, print them out at home and deliver them ;))

PART 3: THE DETAILS

Congratulations! You can pretty much be assured that if you've made it this far, you have an awesome event on your hands.

But you're not done yet.

Now we're going to complete the section on which your chill relies: the organisation. This is the section that will make or break you; that will make the party either come together effortless with total chill, or, if you skip it or mess it up, will have you sobbing in the corner on the morning of the event wondering why you decided to do this in the first place.

Be realistic in this section. Allow more time than you think you'll need, never less. Schedule, schedule, schedule, and everything will come together just fine ☺

STEP 8: RUN SHEET

If this is the kind of party where you're having games or activities, creating a run sheet might take a little more thought—but even if not, you might have speeches or other items, and it's worth just sketching out a super quick order-of-events for your own peace of mind.

A nice, general rule of thumb is:

Activity - eat - activity - cake cutting - activity - dessert - closing activity

(Having the cake cutting BEFORE dessert exponentially increases the likelihood of people actually eating the cake—though I did this with the pirate treasure party AND made a super tiny cake AND still ended up with nearly 3/4 of it left over!)

This rule-of-thumb guide often *averages out* to about half an hour per item, giving a three-hour party—usually a good length. If activities are your focus area you may wish to include more, but keep an eye on how it will impact your time.

Also keep an eye on props that you will need for your activities—you'll add them to the timeline soon :) You can find suggestions for activities in the same place as you found your other ideas—and chances are, you'll already have some great ideas lurking on that brainstorm board you created back in step 3.

For the Toy Story party, the run sheet looked like this:
Pass-the-parcel
Main food
Pin the eyes on the alien
Cake cutting
Mr Potato-Head cupcake decorating
Dessert

And of course, it was at the local park, so there was play equipment around as well.

For the pirate treasure party, we had:
Coconut bowling
Main food
Treasure hunt
Cake cutting
Piñata
Dessert
Opening of presents

For the coconut bowling, we filled up some water bottles with sand, taped a picture of a palm tree on the front, and bought a literal coconut for the kids to use to bowl at them.

The treasure hunt was in place of party bags: each guest was given a list of small items from the dollar store to find in our front yard, and an empty party bag to put them in.

The piñata was constructed by my wonderful mother with the kids out of an old nappy box!

In addition to this, we had the paddling pool, the trampoline (which we scored free from the neighbours, who were moving out on the morning of the party!), and the sandpit out for the kids to play with at any time.

For the magical baby shower, this was the plan:
Peg Game
Main course
Cake cutting
Baby animals guessing game
Dessert
Washcloth teddies
Pass the parcel

STEP 9: BEFORE THE DAY

This is THE crucial step when it comes to keeping your chill and not dying: scheduling in your tasks.

You need two lists here. List one is for food, along with who is going to be responsible for buying or making it, and when they need to buy or make it. The second list is for props (for decorations or activities), again with who is responsible and when it needs to be bought/made. Don't forget to include the cake :)

When thinking about when to do things, it helps to break down each item into its components. For example, making the cake includes:
- Shopping
- Baking the cake
- Shaping, possibly filling, and icing the cake
- Decorating the cake

You could do each of these on a different day if you needed to (and I frequently do with big cakes such as for weddings!), or you could combine steps on days where you have more time (for example, I did everything but shop and bake the treasure chest cake on the Saturday afternoon before the party).

Do the same for food: how far out can you make things? What can you freeze and reheat on the day?

Make sure to consider your timetable in the weeks leading up to the party: what days are you already booked out with other things? What days do you have a lot of time?

Your aim is to spread the food and decoration making back as far as possible, so you have as little to do in the direct lead-up to the party—and definitely as little as possible to do on the day.

So, make your list of everything that needs to be made or bought, figure out how far ahead you can do it, and diarise it. Don't forget to take into account other appointments you have, nights where you know you're already pressed for time, weekends already full of Stuff. Work around that.

Start at the day of the party with things that can only be done on the day, and work backwards from there. You might find you only need to start party prep a week out; or you might find you need to start getting things together a couple of months ahead of time. Better to know that now, and avoid a frantic run-up to Party Day.

Trust me: I know I've said it already, but this is THE step that makes planning amazing parties without dying even possible.

STEP 10: ON THE DAY

By now, everything is just about done. You'll need to actually put up the decorations (if you didn't do that yesterday, or even last week if you have things that will last without getting destroyed—remember, we're all about not dying here, so if the party decorations go up a week early to preserve your chill, GOOD ON YOU. Do what you have to do!), and there will probably be some food prep involved (at the very least you might have to actually place that takeaway order, or something), but everything that can possible be done already will have been, so you'll be going into Party Day with a pretty clear idea of what you need to do.

To help you on the day, you could make a list of everything you'll need to do, and prioritise (and delegate!):

What needs to be done first?

How long will it take?

When can you reasonably start working on various things?

How many people do you have to help out, and what can you get them to do?

Make that list, and also a list of anything else you need to remember on the day (there may or may not be anything), while you're doing your planning. That way, on the day, all you need to do is follow your last list, then sit back, relax, and enjoy the party!

Just remember that like any good battle, no plan survives first contact with the enemy: if something's not working on the day, don't fight it. That's a guaranteed way to lose your chill and end up dead.

Instead, adapt. You have a whole Pinterest board of ideas; you know what the important focus of the party is; you know what your idea kernel is. Nothing else matters. Roll with it.

And remember, the 'partee' will probably have a fabulous time anyway (and they'll have a better time with you chill and not dead than they will if you're dead of stress and terror).

Case in point: In 2016, kiddo had a Frozen party, because he was totally obsessed with the movie. Cakes are my thing, right? So I had this fantastic cake planned, with pale blue toffee shards, and blue icing, and a topper of Elsa and Anna that one of the grandparents was providing.

On the day, the toffee shards went cloudy, the cake was crumbly and the crumbs kept getting in the icing because I hadn't allowed myself time to do a crumb coat before icing it properly, and the cake topper went missing.

I, the one for whom cakes are The Focus, served up a cake whose icing was bespeckled with crumbs, with weird-looking suspicious toffee shards, and a topper cut out of a themed paper plate. And you know what?

Kiddo loved it. It was perfect. There were Elsa and Anna in their ice castle, and his imagination filled in the rest.

And because I'd consciously decided to Not Die, I was able to laugh at my ridiculous, imperfect cake even while I was making a mess of it—and a grand time was had by all :) (Plus I had a great reminder about the need to plan adequate cake-decorating time! :D)

CONCLUSION

So there you have it: ten easy steps to planning an amazing, Pinterest-worthy party without dying or losing your chill. I've been using these steps for a few years now, refining them each time, and when I made the planning sheets so I could use them for the latest party in early 2018, WOW did that make a difference. I think it literally took an hour to plan the entire party (although as aforementioned, some of that changed when I raided my sister's props cupboard).

If your party doesn't come together quite the way you wanted the first time, that's okay! First of all, it was probably awesome anyway, even if it was a bit different to how you planned.

And secondly, like anything, the more you practise something, the better you get at it. Keep practising, and before you know it, you'll have people asking YOU how on earth you manage to plan such amazing parties without losing your chill—or even ending up dead. :)

And don't forget to check out the printable worksheets at the end of the book!

WORKSHEETS

There are printable worksheets at the end of this book for you to use when planning your own parties. If, for some reason, you have difficulty printing them out, head to:

http://www.inkprintpress.com/books/books-by-genre/non-fiction/pinterest-party-planning/party-planning-worksheets/ to download them as a pdf.

Use the coupon code PARTY101 to get them for free. (The coupon will only work once.)

SUPPORTERS

With thanks to my amazing Patreon supporters, Clare, Thea and Bethy <3

https://www.patreon.com/amylaurens

ABOUT THE AUTHOR

AMY LAURENS is secretly a superhero.

HA! She wishes! That would definitely make it easier to get done the epic number of things on her daily to-do list.

Instead, she's actually just an ordinary person who happens to be pretty good at organising. Being a high-school teacher, a mum, a multi-small business owner, and somewhat of a habitual overachiever will kind of do that to you.

Either that, or it will break you. Amy's been there done that too. On balance, she recommends hyper-organisation as a life strategy, compared to monthly breakdowns.

Or, you know, you could just not try to be amazing at everything all at once. That's probably the more sensible option.

...Sensible people never have any fun.

You can contact Amy at:
amyllaurens@gmail.com
www.amylaurens.com
https://www.patreon.com/amylaurens

Party Planning

Focus Area
- Cake
- Food
- Decorations
- Games/Activities
- Something else: _____

Idea Kernel

General idea: _____

Specific focus: _____

Keeper Ideas:
(from your brainstorm)

_____   _____
_____   _____
_____   _____
_____   _____
_____   _____
_____   _____
_____   _____
_____   _____

www.amylaurens.com

Party Planning

Remember

We're trying to do this WITHOUT dying, so unless decorations are your focus area, you can totally get away with just decorating the table.

Remember to get your money's worth out of the cake: include it in your decorating plan as a centrepiece for the table!

Decorations

Backdrop: _____
_____

Height element: _____
_____

Front element: _____
_____

Other: _____
_____

Party Planning

Consider

How many people are you feeding?
How much time will you have to cook in the month prior?
How much time will you have to cook on the day?
How many people do you have to help, both before and on the day?
Will you link the food into the theme, and if so, how?

Savoury Menu

Main: _____
_____

Side 1: _____
_____

Side 2: _____
_____

Side 3: _____
_____

Dessert Menu

Main: _____
_____

Side 1: _____
_____

Side 2: _____
_____

Side 3: _____
_____

Party Planning

Cake!

General description of cake:
_____
_____
_____

Details:

Who is making? _____

Number of serves: _____

Flavours: _____
_____
_____

Icing: _____

Decorations:

_____
_____
_____
_____
_____
_____
_____
_____

Party Planning

Guest List:

Party Planning

Things to Remember

A nice, general rule of thumb is:
activity – eat – activity – cake cutting – activity – dessert – (activity)

- Cutting the cake before dessert means you won't have mountains of leftover cake because everyone's too full to eat it!
- This rule-of-thumb guide often averages out to about half hour per item, giving a three-hour party.
- If activities are your focus area, you might want to include a few more, but be aware of how that will impact your time.

Run Sheet:

Food Planner

FOOD ITEM	WHO'S MAKING/BUYING IT	WHEN TO MAKE/BUY IT

Decoration/Activity Planner

DECORATION/ACTIVITY/PROP	WHO'S MAKING/BUYING IT	WHEN TO MAKE/BUY IT

www.amylaurens.com

Party Planning

Things to Remember

On The Day:
(approximate timeline)

_____   _____
_____   _____
_____   _____
_____   _____
_____   _____
_____   _____
_____   _____

www.ingramcontent.com/pod-product-compliance
Lightning Source LLC
Chambersburg PA
CBHW050447010526
44118CB00013B/1722